Chameleon Moon

Chameleon Moon

Poems by

Antonia Clark

Published by Bellevue Books

ISBN 978-1-7336142-0-7

In memory of my parents,
Ebbie and Sophie,
and my sister, Barbara Jo.

And for Tomcat with all my love.
Thank you for so many years
of love and laughter.

Acknowledgments

Many thanks to the editors of the journals in which these poems, or earlier versions of them, were first published.

14 by 14, The 2River View, Apparatus Magazine, Autumn Sky Poetry, Avatar Review, Ballard Street Poetry Journal, Big Toe Review, Camroc Poetry Press, The Centrifugal Eye, The Chimaera, The Commonline Journal, Contemporary American Voices, The Cortland Review, Eclectica Magazine, Flutter Poetry Journal, The Fox Chase Review, Glass: A Journal of Poetry, Gutter Eloquence Magazine, Innisfree Poetry Journal, Lily, Loch Raven Review, Lucid Rhythms, The Pedestal Magazine, Quay, Rattle, Red Fez, Softblow, Soundzine, Stirring, Victorian Violet, Zocalo Press.

Special Thanks

To *Eclectica Magazine* for publishing so many of my poems, including the one that gives this volume its name.

To Lauren Everett Finn, whose beautiful painting, "Moondance," graces the cover.

To Jude Goodwin, for founding The Waters, where almost all of these poems began.

To all my writing buddies at The Beach for the camaraderie and support. And thanks to whoever brought the margaritas!

Poems

Smoke and Mirrors

Dawn in the Glass House

Amends

Smoke and Mirrors

Sisterhood

Rebecca and Rachel. Those were the names
we wanted, instead of the ones we had.
I taught her how to tie her boxy brown
corrective shoes, to tell time, do times tables,
tell when the coast was clear, to tiptoe,
lie, create a stir, slip out unnoticed.

The cellar smelled of musty rags, dusty jars.
We waited there for signs, for coded messages
from Ethan Allen and the Green Mountain Boys,
and later, from Frankie Pascarelli, Billy Cutts,
waited to be rescued, to fall, weak and sighing,
into their arms behind the furnace.

We turned forbidden words on our tongues
like sour lemon drops, words we dreamed
of saying to those boys. We scrawled them
on slips of paper, dared one another to slide
them into locked drawers, under closet doors.

When parents found them, we learned
to think fast, run faster, always imagining
worse disaster. At night, we held each other
and shivered, pretending we were the sisters
in the news who'd fallen into a well.

Upstate

By midsummer, the unmowed grass
waved long and silver in the wind,
rippling like water. Behind the house,
far away from the devil's claw
and horsetail tea, the lingering odor
of camphor salve, I'd dive in, lie flat
on the buzzy bottom, breathing hard,
my good ear pressed to the ground.

A feral cat trailed my grandmother
room to room, invisible and terrifying
and ready to scratch your eyes out.
Sometimes, I heard it hissing.
My grandmother pursed her lips,
said now hush, that's just the kettle.
But I knew she'd seen it.
Seen it and fed it meat.

She carried her frightening belly
before her, sang battle hymns
under her breath. Her own spit
could keep coydogs away.
She called my mother the Queen,
said there's no use wishing
you could churn sour milk into sweet,
wishing your sons had more sense.

She dragged away the concrete
cistern lid so I could hear the banshee
that lived down there, held me
by the neck like a scrawny kitten,
pushed me toward the blackness, then
pulled me back from the edge. A shroud
of dampness wreathed my shoulders.
Below us, water dripped, tinny and cold.

4

Underwater

In the house of green rooms,
we learned to be wary, children
in a family of poor swimmers.

We studied the mermaid painted
on the wall above the tub: emerald
scales shimmering, seaweed
tangled in her dazzling hair.

We practiced swimming from room,
to room, hiding in shallows, sliding
around corners like the shadows of fish.

At bedtime we begged for tales
of shipwrecks and drownings.
And later, we dreamed of oceans,
rising and falling in our element,
without needing to hold our breath.

Home Permanent

My mother was the one who wanted curls
on me, so I was made to sit, straight-backed
and still, on catalogs stacked on a chair.
She wound my hair relentlessly around
the plastic rods we'd sorted out by size,
pulled so tight tears stung my eyes. The thin
pink lotion burned my scalp, dripped in my ears.
Complaining only makes it worse, she said.
She'd learned that lesson well enough, herself.
She said to hold my head up, not to squirm
or whine. She said she'd prayed that I'd be born
with natural curl, but I was cursed with hair
like hers. All of our lives, we'd have to take
pains, and suffer, suffer for beauty's sake.

Easter

For the photo, you take your still-life place,
cross-legged on the play-table, in a starched
pink peony dress, a straw basket in your lap.
Your sister's bawling her head off, afraid
of the camera, the tripod, mothballed Mr. Otis,
who made house calls like a country doctor,
dragging along his black bag, his bent leg,
breathing his horehound breath.

Your mother keeps trying to get it right,
moves in and out of the frame, coaxing,
cajoling, recombing your sister's damp hair.
Your father stands apart, considering
the painted trout that hangs above your head,
a single silver muscle arcing over the rainbow
water, how it is caught in a net of light,
how such a moment can hook you for life.

They are all dead, the photo lost, the trout
plunged into the icy stream. You keep reeling
it back, the sweet smell of cellophane grass
and chocolate eggs, the scratch of stiff petticoats,
the old photographer's bobbing head: hold still,
smile, freeze. The flash and the blackness after.
No sound but your sister crying and crying,
the catch in her throat as she gasps for air.

Christmas with Event Horizon

My mother is singing "Wśród Nocnej Ciszy,"
but I have forgotten the words.
And there is a pot of barszcz, and uszka,
though no recorded recipes remain.
Aunt Agnieszka, her shiny black dress
stretched across bosom and bottom,
has come and taken over the kitchen,
all wide hips and doughy arms, shooing
me out of her way. She raises a finger
to her lips while tipping a thimble
of "medicine" into her tea. Mrs. Brzezinski
has brought the raisin pie. My sister and I
take our turns rubbing our cheeks
on her fur coat, bristling cold from outside.
She hands out candy canes, bought
at a bargain price last year. She holds
them over our heads and we jump up
and down, grabbing and laughing. Later,
we'll stash them in a paper bag, with the last
of the Halloween candy, the hard stuff
no one wants. The mistletoe hangs
in the archway, Mom and Dad avoiding
it when they pass. The tree in its usual
corner, a tiny crèche almost hidden
beneath it, the wise men and sheep
kneeling outside. My sister and I
have walked them through miles of pine
needle forests and fields of artificial snow
to arrive exhausted at the manger, squabbling
over who should stand closest to the baby.
And all of us now take our ritual places
after Mass as if with purpose, as if for posterity—
my father with his harmonica and red hat,
mother ensconced in her tapestry rocker
with a steaming mug, a plate of pork pie.

My sister arranging the presents to make
a perfect picture, the way I'll always see it.
My own slender fingers, now those
of a stranger, smoothing the ribbon
of a shining bow before I pull it loose.

Widow's Weeds

Mornings, the widow sets the house to rights,
sweeps a feather duster over the maple dresser,
clatters his empty hangers and recalls
bare branches, bones.

She polishes her collection of grievances,
lines them up like figurines on the mantel,
each a familiar shape to hold onto,
to turn in her hands.

Behind closed doors, she keeps to her rounds,
holds her ground. Surely, he'd not want her
letting things go, as if all their years of strife
had meant nothing.

Woman Waiting

She ignores clocks and calendars,
lets time slip through her fingers.

One summer, she ran barefoot
all the way to Hartland, a love note

clutched in her fist, her hair like fire
taken by wind, a thin cotton skirt

clinging to her bare legs. So easy,
then, to question perfect strangers

about birth, blood, to keep faith
with her own body's deep secrets.

Now, she smoothes a polyester
housedress over her soft belly,

drags a comb through coarse
white hair without need of a mirror.

She holds the future in her mouth,
a pill hidden under her tongue,
and refuses to swallow.

Unfinished Marilyn

I dreamed of her for years, the portrait
my father painted from *Playboy*'s centerfold.
Before things got out of hand, my mother
banished them both, Dad and his sultry
mistress, to the cellar. He'd spend evenings
stroking an arm, softening her gaze.
Perhaps he saw there what he could lose,
grappling with her hard mystery. He gave
her up, put away his brushes for good.

She was the last thing we found, when we
cleaned out the house. Damp and moldy,
she was stashed behind shelves of canning
jars against the cement wall. For decades,
she'd knelt there, shivering, one too-long
arm bent painfully behind her head, skin
blotchy, her dull hair only underpainted.

I packed the jars into a box for the dump.
Their dusky contents, once peaches or yams,
bobbed in syrup. I glanced at her, propped
against the wall in a shaft of late sun,
awkward and ordinary and tired of it all,
and saw, for the first time, that she had
my mother's eyes. Dry leaves rustled
in the window-well and the crimson curtain
behind her rippled in a trick of light.

In Another City

The yellow moon, the factories, brief snow—
I'm only passing through aboard a train
streaking through your night, Once, long ago,
in another dingy city, in light rain,
I lingered at the station with some lover
or other, someone arriving or departing—
both of us young and destined to discover
absence. The old story's always starting
or ending. And the chapters in between
slip by like nameless towns along the way.
The drifting moon and snow, a view I've seen
a hundred times. A woman dressed in gray
waits on the platform. I notice, as we pass,
my own face through the window's misted glass.

Of an Evening

The backyard's an overturned cup, full
of insect hum, earth's murmur and spin.

Leaves stir and submit, a woman's
sigh at day's end, a leavening.

My mother disapproved of wishing
for more or wishing time away.

If she had regrets, she kept them
harbored, hushed, and refrained

from counting heavenly bodies
or counting on them. But tonight,

I see more stars than ever, no matter
how many they tell me have died.

I lean toward them, into darkness, feet
barely anchored on the tilting planet.

My mother sighed to let the world
move through her, an easing,

an opening, in which some small animal
might startle, then disappear into the trees.

Orthopedics

I've heard how easily bones break,
disintegrate, how hard they are to build,
set right. You hear, every day,
of bad backs that will never give up
their pain no matter how strong the rods
of steel the spine is made to bear,
of crippled limbs, arthritic hands,
diseases that knob and hobble.
An old woman has a hold on me,
leaches my calcium day by day,
cackles that she'll steal my finger joints,
crack my ribs, one by one. She lays
her bony hand along my skull,
taking my full measure, biding her time.

Why My Body

Because I've made it a temple
and worshipped at its altar.

Because I've stuffed it with secrets
and let it make me sorry.

Because it can't follow directions,
a slave to delay and meander.

Because I've tried to conceal it,
desiring the bodies of others.

Because I've scraped and scarred it,
teaching it needless lessons.

Because it's the seed of my father,
freighted with silent mutations.

Because it's the flesh of my mother
and nothing can please or appease it.

Because it burns up my ambition
and expels the ashes of failure.

Because it grows soft and loose-fitting,
mocking my ministrations.

Because of the rust and the scratches,
the ominous knock in its ribcage.

Because of the thorn in its rouged cheek,
the taste of blood in its mouth.

Because I'll always resent it
and always have to love it.

About the Dead

What children understand about the dead
is how they cling to life, how they assert
their sentiments and preferences, instead
of giving up the ghost. Children, alert
to stirrings of the air, to whispers, hushed
voices in the kitchen, strain to hear
their soft footfalls. The dead cannot be rushed
into the afterlife. They linger near
their loved ones, listening and leaving clues—
a bar of yellow light across the floor,
scents of earth and river, muddy shoes,
missing change, the creaking of a door.
They wait for signs, longing for us to mention
their names, insatiable for our attention.

Comedian

This is serious, they keep saying,
no laughing matter. But he can't stop.
Even when it hurts to breathe. Irony
being both beautiful and humorous.

He lines the bottles up on the sill
over the sink, the pills in a row
on the table, pushes them
into a smile, then a scowl.

Most are small and pastel. Only
one that's hard to get down,
huge and oblong and furious yellow.
I can cut it in half for you, she says.

But he says, leave it. Let me
choke on it. Killed by the cure—
Now that would be funny.

Diagnosis

The evidence is always flimsy,
shadowy images, vague imaginings—

the body's secret history: stones
lodged in crooks and shallows,
scarred fields, accumulated debris.

On its red and blue map—
clogged thruways, weedy back roads
streaming with illegal aliens.

A haunting of drawn breath,
turbulent with rasp and wheeze—

the scrape and catch of a key
in its lock, a turning, the dark
and empty room beyond.

Smoke and Mirrors

My sister dressed in the colors of water
and stone, walked out on foggy mornings
in search of misted rivers,
folded herself into low-lying clouds.

She insisted that none of this
was for the purpose of deception.
It's a matter of becoming

accustomed, she said. It's incremental.

She studied the art of graceful sleight:
To take her leave without notice, without
a visible stirring of air, as if dying
were only another illusion.

The hard part is what to do with the body,
she told me. The rest is nothing.
It's easy to disappear.

Famous Last Words

The dying make no bones about it. It's life
they want to talk about — business as usual:
news and weather, sports. The sound of rain
striking the windowpane, the most recent hole in one,
stock prices, interest rates, errands to run.

The dying talk of elephants, veal pies, rising fog,
tiresome wallpaper, shore birds at low tide. Chekhov
spoke fondly of champagne, Bogart of Scotch,
Dylan Thomas totted up his whiskeys, satisfied.
They often speak of the dark or ask for the light
to be left on or off. They may cry out,
"I'm still alive!" or more soberly reflect
on things they should have done or said,
bills still unpaid, books left unread.

My father, a joker even at the end,
said "Don't call me, I'll call you." It's kept
the thought of him alive, it's true. Hope springs
eternal, just like fear, each time the phone rings.

The Bridge, When We Came to It

We finally came to that bridge
we'd talked about for years,
never really believing in it.
Yet it rose up all at once
before us, suspended, shining
like a cherished illusion.
We'd never really wanted
to cross, but when we came
to it, there was no way
to turn back.

We finally came to that bridge,
later than expected, bent
with burdens. We crossed
in silence, tipping our faces
to the north wind, listening
to the creak of cables,
the girders' groan.
Far below us, the water lay
black as the night, crowded
with floating stars.

Coming of Age in the Physical World

My mother's hazel eyes, my father's look
of surprise, my sister's braided hair
in a locked chest.

The force and rate of change, a reaction
for every act or notion, a sense
of endless motion.

Their bodies at rest.

Dawn in the Glass House

The Third Night

The lake held fast to its huge and stubborn silence.
Searchers slumped on the edges of beds,
while wives rubbed their backs and sobbed.

The bass line from Tutti's thumped
over the water, dragging a wake of revving
engines, an occasional starburst of angry shouts.

We drifted in and out of the drowned girl's
story, damp sand gritty on my back, and even
as I moved under your rough hands,

I claimed her body, submitting to the waves,
cornsilk hair streaming, limbs some man
had once pinned to the ground, rising, falling free.

Dawn in the Glass House

To recall the audible ice, the creaking lake,
the way you stood rigid at the window
waiting for everything to break apart

is reminder enough. The old decade
had begun to come undone, a threadbare
robe slipped from my empty arms.

No need to delve into reasons, recount
unjust demands. That morning, I read
your answers in the set of your shoulders.

Shivering in milky half-light, I burned up
my questions like dry kindling, fed them
one by one to the leaky, smoking stove.

Sleepwalker

You'll always be uncertain of footing, always
startle when a cat squalls like a dying man.

If you stand absolutely still, you can hear
everything giving way, giving in, the slow

wave of night washing the edge of the lawn,
leaves turning up their hands in defeat,

the cascade of pebbles as the known world
tilts on its axis. You could shuffle through

your whole life like this, groping for doorways,
feeling your way from one question

to the next. The thought of it makes you pray
for insomnia, beg like a child for a light left burning.

Afternoon Rain

Clouds hunch and shudder, slope-shouldered
lovers who once crowded like children over
a handful of pebbles, slick from the river.

The kitchen fills with yellow light. Voices
fall away. When it comes, the rain wavers
on the glass, gathers, then gushes all at once.

A woman holds back the truth of her life
as long as she's able, then spills everything,
learns that she's always been insatiable.

Now she will stop at nothing
and there's nothing left to stop her.

Illogical

The answers are too easy,
too eager to give you
what you want — a touch
in the dark, honey and heat.

How many times must you
lose your head, mistake
promise for premise,
come-on for conclusion?

You drop your defenses
like articles of clothing
at any earnest argument,
any tanned and muscular

rationale, forgetting to ask
for something in return,
forgetting the way you'll
regret it later, the way

the answers come begging
for attention, turning
your head, twisting your arm,
before the questions.

Everyday Arithmetic

I have finally figured out
how you do your math—
numbers scribbled on the backs
of envelopes, paper bags.
Your balance sheet
of insinuations, grievances
totted up like daily expenses.
You square X and Y, divide
one lie by another and pretend
it comes out even.

I am your problem to solve.
Each night, you whisper
the same formulas
against my neck, fingers busy,
tracing equations, pressing
upon me your need to know,
to master, to make me
yield up one right answer.

Punctuation

I am a woman who has learned
to appreciate punctuation — the sweet
shy comma, a barely audible whisper,
the curl of a wet tongue in your ear
before you're pulled into the flow;

who succumbs to semicolons,
to the throb of breathlessness
at that almost end-stopped pause;
when you know there's more to come —
and then the coming undone;

who cannot overlook any colon's
brisk insistence, its bold demand:
this is going to be important.
Listen up: if you miss this, everything
up until now will have been in vain;

or the finality, the fearlessness
of periods. They tell it like it is.
This really is the end, my girl.
No use crying. Any moment,
you'll begin again, delve
into a new sentence,
a whole new story.

Direct Object

A sentence longs to climax,
cannot lie unresponsive,
while you go through the motions,
putting one word after another.
This isn't bricklaying
we're talking about.
You can't disguise rising action
with a string of prepositional
phrases, hoping to keep the lid on.
A verb isn't really interested
in stroking, endearments,
your slow stoking of the fire.
A verb needs to get down
to business. A verb is dying
to find the object of its desire
and come blasting through
to the conclusion, to have done,
to have completed the action
and left you satisfied. Period.

Taking the I Out of the Poem

A muddle of nameless objects, mindless acts,
a random heap of odd-shaped artifacts.
A box of photos in an antique store—
faces no one remembers anymore.
A yard-sale jumble, useless odds and ends—
a pair of glasses with a missing lens,
rusted tools and nails, a plaid wool suit,
broken toys, a bowl of plastic fruit.
Questions with no answers but clichés,
a puzzle with no exit from its maze.
A life without a sense of history,
a scrim of shadow play and mystery
without the fabric of connective tissue—
An absence so profound no one will miss you.

The Tool for the Task

You don't expect a poem to be a knife
or even bread. At most, a glass of wine.
If blade makes you think grass,
you have nothing but grass to cut, sun
to spill. For bread, you go to the baker,
you glue together clumsy wings for flight.

You could be anywhere—an autumn orchard,
a subway, standing at a counter,
a smoky back room, studying discards—
when glancing light cuts through still air,
when a blade-shaped word slices the air.

On the wrong side of the river, a bridge
could be just what you need. In your head
the idea of bridge pulls the far shore close.
On the strength of it, you cross into dusk.

Take a notion and necessary objects show
up to serve it. Would you turn right? A corner
comes to life. Out of nowhere, a boathouse.

Here's the thing you've always needed to know:
It's the language of levers that moves the world,
a dialect of hammers that nails down its roof.

But don't expect a sign, a map, a star.
Go the way of danger, assassins in every alley.
Move now. Leave your glass on the table.

If you need shelter, conjure trees.
If you grow thirsty, a cup.

When what you need is a knife,
when all you can think of is a knife,
then the poem becomes a knife.
Then you have no use for wine.

Compass

1

As if there were a map
tattered but legible

I take this to be
a road trip.

Diners and dives
miles out of the way

in a dry county.

2

I want the next
rest stop, the way

I want the slow
waltz, the soft bed—

if only for a night

as if they signified
in a secret language.

Sky Cover

I remember now, how a hand can open,
palm to sky, as if checking for rain
or asking for an answer. It's the hand
I recall when you talk of change, beg one
more favor. A hand with nothing to give.

A woman learns early to read the weather,
knows what's coming after hard kisses
and swift release — even if, under the certainty
of gathered clouds, she lets you believe
for the moment that it's clearing in the east.

Chameleon Moon

On some fall days, you could smell the fires
everywhere. Backyard leaf piles, rubbish in rusted
metal drums, smoldering tires at Ratty's junkyard.

At night, smoke drifted over the roofs, seeped
into windows and dreams with news of bombed
cities, midnight arsonists, flames that licked slyly

along baseboards or leapt from kitchen cupboards.
Wind scurried ashes along the streets and gutters.
And the chameleon moon blinked its liquid eye.

We shivered in the heat, kicked free of the sheets
and pulled them up again. We turned to our lovers
and turned away at the touch of burning flesh.

Dénouement

What passes for plot is merely
an accrual of non sequiturs,
a scatter of snapshots: a woman
crying at her wedding, a riptide
in the bay, a battered copy
of *Madame Bovary* by the bed.

Effects slip free of causes as easily
as lovers slip away in the night.
A woman's tears might as well be
brought on by rain, her fate
determined by constellations
of stars or starlings.

Endings, surprising but inevitable,
leave you with nothing
but retrospect — in which motives
suddenly clamor for attention:
why the groom always seemed
a little suspect, why you've avoided
the ocean for decades, why all
you recall, after taking an entire
summer to read the book,
is sex and poison.

Sequence

One thing follows another. Starlings pick
at the backyard grass, and down the street
someone starts up a mower, blasts
through morning's muzzy haze.
Thunderheads haul their massive bellies
across the valley and stockpots boil over.
Wallpaper, newly hung, resists adhesion,
slides down the walls like cast-off clothing.
At night, the train's long whistle shrills
from the trestle, an answer to all
your unasked questions and, beside you,
your lover's breathing catches like a rusty hinge,
for no particular reason, then regains its rhythm.

Precautions

All winter we spent quiet evenings,
hunched over game boards, clicking tokens
square to square, scratching scores
on the backs of envelopes.

Word games always made me feel
we'd quarreled. You'd slap down *pretense,*
and I knew it meant nothing. Even so,
I'd play *defensive,* save letters for *insinuate.*

Outside, snow and sirens, red beams
sweeping the bellies of clouds. Sighs
slipped free of us like shed illusions.
We'd quit before either of us lost.

Later I trailed you from room to room,
while you checked lights and locks,
listening for the distant crack of thunder,
gunfire, shattering glass.

Attired

My evening wear, like my underwear,
isn't really silk, merely silky. And my fur,
merely furry. I'm in the midst
of a makeover, an unfinished wish,
not yet fit for conversation. I can't say
where this will lead, resist speaking

engagements. Most of my thoughts
are proprietary, like my body, subject
to arcane privacy laws. Even so,
it's rumored that I've grown morose,
remotely disgruntled. Hunkered

down, I flaunt my wordlessness, wear it
like the newest fashion, cowl collar
pulled high to hide my mouth.
It covers the bare skin of unknowing.
Perhaps the attire of a higher calling.
With nothing to reveal, I'm stone
cold, granite in winter. *Say nothing,*
says my muffler. *Hush,* my fuzzy gloves.

Hidden Identity

Paralyzed by lights that spring out
of nowhere, you're caught in the trap

of the liminal. Never at home in your own
skin. Searching for your animal.

Night things twitch, skitter. Swish
of tail, scrape of nails.

You could touch yourself in the dark,
find claws, talons, scales.

The disease of living eats us up.
Sleep is a bed of lies.

Any morning, you could wake to bone,
hide, holes where once were eyes.

Fugue

Here and not here, there and not there.
A fugitive, I've grown wings, grown
into anonymity, become unknown.

A season in transition. Call me April
or May. A traveler without a past. Call me
tabula rasa. Call me running scared.

My name's a holy text, a password,
a ticket to an unnamed destination,
clutched in my fist like a stone.

Call me Nomad, call me Peregrine.
Call me wanderer, witch, no one you know.
My name's a hollow note, a shifting wind,

cloud shadow on water, the glittering eye
of the crow, a dark bird in my throat
and stranger, I'm trying to let it go.

Blind Faith

Everyone knows the moon
has a habit of lying, making
promises it can never keep.

Some things we give ourselves
up to, as easily as to sleep,
however suspect, however brief.

Even as we know that beauty
twists the wrist of logic,
that desire suspends disbelief.

Amends

In a Village to the North

You begin to think of him again
in a northern town, and surely,
a small town where people speak softly
in foreign accents is a place where
you'll always feel helpless. There,
each sentence takes days to arrive,
a slow train winding through the valley,
carrying its cargo of lost hours.

You shop for simple things, potatoes
or apples, and think of how you'll pare
and prepare them. You take them
up whole, like memories you cannot bear
to set aside, and turn and turn them,
searching for the blemish, the bruise.

How can it matter whether you see him
again. Either way, you will continue
struggling through the same sentence.
Giving up, you offer the shopkeeper
a handful of change, let him take
whatever you owe. The train whistle
drifts over the fields. There's no
straight line between past and future.

Shades of Gray

Swollen clouds rolling in,
thunder complaining to the west.
Cat shadow. Mouse tail.
Skin of the limp mackerel
in a dented tin pail.
The damp wool coat of dusk.
Dull sheen of an old man's eyes
brimming with gratitude.
The dead woman's sweater
folded on a shelf.
The wolf. The distance.

Rapprochement

I agreed to put aside the ruined vacation
and he agreed to put aside the slips
in bookkeeping. I admitted that some
of my friends were not the best company—
were, now that I thought of it, intolerable.
And he admitted that his mother had never
liked me from day one. I observed
that everyday objects often intrude
on our best intentions and he offered
that no one should be held accountable
for where the dust settles. The henhouse,
we agreed, might have welcomed
the fox, the window might have shattered,
anyway, without human intervention.
Effects can spring into being like rabbits
out of a hat, their causes nowhere to be seen.
Just as, in darkness, bodies turn naturally
to one another without need for reason.

Secret Sharer

Pain pauses in passing to tip its hat, to single
you out with a wink and nod. You're bound
in an alliance you want no part of.

The way the devil reminds you of the pact,
even though you claim to have forgotten it.

The way the dentist tosses off pleasantries,
asks what kind of music you like, before
he sets about drilling and grinding.

Your mother warned you long ago, told you
what would happen when your father got home.
You can't pretend not to know what's coming.

Marseille

You draw a map of France
on my back and I ask you
to scratch, there, somewhere
near Avignon, perhaps where
we visited the abbey, plucked
fresh figs from the trees,
and sipped the Farigoule—
but you've gone on ahead
to Marseille, incandescent
in the sun, its deep blue
irresistible waters. I am lost,
rocking in the swell, as you
touch, there and there and there,
every bright boat in the bay.

Navigator

It falls to me, a woman with no sense
of direction, to trace the route,

call out the turns and junctions, finger
on the map, eyes watering in wind.

We hoopskirt the cities, aim for wayside
towns — every gulch, gore, gully.

Your eyes swerve to my bare foot
on the hot dash tapping out a signal:

take us down a dusty track, into the high
grass, yield to the lazy buzzing heat.

You take me, make me your compass,
even though you know I'm winging it.

Maps, worn at the creases, tear apart
in my hands, flap from the window like birds.

Let There Be Light

Until they turned off the power, we lit
the place up like a Vegas starship,

a blazing last exuberant blast before
the collapse.

Lighten up, we said, to anyone who objected.
It's a party, man. Like, a party.

Someone's brother brought more bulbs
and extension cords

and the Sunshine Girls got busy
with spotlights and strobes.

When the police arrived, they immediately called
for backup, surrounded the place

and Jesus, it was gorgeous—
all those flashing cherries and blues.

We were dizzy with power, with the whole
goddamn electric spectacle. We were glowing

like radium eaters. The house was an orgy
of brilliance, a solar flare, a red giant.

it was all we'd ever really wanted:
To banish the dark with a flick of the switch.

Lunatic Blues

There was a lunar eclipse that night and we watched
from the meadow.
There was a lunar eclipse, but we could see, through
cloud shadow,
the fat copper penny of moon, shrouded like a widow.

Everyone milled around, waiting, as if Jesus were
going to appear.
Everyone waited, shivering, as if the meaning of life
would come clear.
It was November, below freezing, what were we doing
out there?

We'd heard that the president had lied; it was a matter
of state.
Some thought he could be forgiven, so much to keep
straight—
taxes, war. Others said no excuses. It's already too late.

The thing is, the president said, insane people out there
want to kill every last one of us. They're crazy, filled
with despair,
hatred, evil. That's what insanity is. We must stay
vigilant, aware.

Slowly, the moon shed her garments as in an exotic
burlesque. The moon shed her garments. It was somehow
erotic.
Some kids sang a country-western song, vaguely patriotic.

You gave me that look: we're the last two sane people
on earth.
You gave me that look and I kissed you. Our goddess
of mirth,
the moon, trailing her gauzy dress, smiled for what
it was worth.

A man behind us smirked and said "You gotta get
your kicks."
And we laughed, though everything we love is dying
and there's no fix.
Laughed till we cried, like there was no tomorrow.
Like lunatics.

Opera Nights

That icy season in rented rooms,
days of pale and watery light,
we might have lost one another

if not for how, each night, we listened
through papered walls to her aria
of despair, the heavy strains
of his grievances

how, without a libretto,
we followed the convoluted weave
of their lies and disguises, the songs
of the foolish, the faithless—
he always accusing, demanding,
she promising, pleading

how, in the interlude, we'd turn
to one another, breathless
with their need, their desperate longing

how, in our release, we cried out
with him, *Non so piu cosa son!*
I no longer know who I am!

how in the end, we sobbed
with her, *Lascia ch'io pianga.*
Let me weep, oh, let me weep.

Optical Aberrations and Other Anomalies

Apparent motion can be
a trick of light.

The displacement of stars,
a blurring at the edge
of sight.

The way the angle of rain
changes as you move
through it.

Properties of aquamarine,
and those you bring
to it.

Refraction, reflection,
a slick sideslip between

what we know and guess,
between the seer
and the seen.

The sleights of art,
illusions wrought
by the practiced dancer,

the deflection of a question
that has no answer.

Bear in Mind

It's dangerous to forget the place
the bear calls home, or from what hill
the wolf howls.

It's rain that makes you worry
over what's lost, but ice that brings
the shudder of certainty.

Who has not seen the pilgrims
trampled, the faithful fallen
before the dogs of doubt

or learned too late how cleanly
the metallic blade of logic cuts
through a lifetime of misconception?

One day you're contemplating
shades of gray and the next,
it's ashes to ashes.

One day you hear a tapping
in the attic, and the next
the thundering of hooves.

The dripping faucet augurs
the flood, the broken connection
a world of gaps and lapses.

If the gull cries thrice, can grief
be far behind?

Maybe You Should Write Down
What I Say

You say that when you try
to wake me, I'm reluctant,
slip back into the dream,

a drowning woman who refuses
a lifeline. So often,

morning feels like a bruise
on the eyelids, first light
the flash of a blade.

I'm afraid to leave
unfinished business,
dangling modifiers
whole cities of bright ideas.

You ease me back,
as if from the chasm's edge,
tell me I'm talking
nonsense, or maybe
not nonsense, you say,
maybe a poem.

A House Climbs a Hill

I like the way a house climbs a hill,
the hill rounding its shoulders
like a man stooping
to let a child climb aboard.

The way the house clings, stands
upright, the way the child straddles
and rides high, unafraid.

The way I rode on my father's
rounded shoulders, waving
to the world spread out below,
hills and houses waiting
for a new word to rise to my lips.
A gold wand in my hand.

This house, this hill, this man.
The way we bend, bear, shoulder
one another, moment to moment.

Amends

Regret lingers, niggles. Yellow lilies
on the table, gone brown in the vase.
The garden we talk about, endlessly,
but never begin, deterred by tough sod.

On the edge of the walk, the wheelbarrow
full of stones waits like an undelivered
apology. Within, the floor needs scrubbing
and only hands and knees will do the job.

I know that forgiveness is a simple meal—
a salad, a boiled potato, a glass of tea.
Easy to prepare, to offer. That the silence
afterward will satisfy, perhaps even nourish.

The Antonym of Rain

There are no entries
for the antonym of rain.

More than mere aridity:
a gentle ascending

what rises from the bodies
of the dead, what nearly

undoes us, but keeps us
from becoming undone

restoring dust to our windows
haze to the cleansed air

a necessary condition
between sorrow and relief.

Dear Tendril

Petiole, part leaf, part stem,
rootlike thread, hair of the vine,
you twist any trellis, twine
around whatever you touch,

tenacious.

Slender tentacle,
nothing but coil and spiral,
grabbing the branch,
grasping the straw.

All you can do, like any of us
is clutch and climb,
clasp and cling,

hold on.

Sleeping Bear

The night's a great black bear
that smells of grease and sleep.

No twinkling lights, no kerosene lamp
at the mouth of the cave. We tiptoe.

Not even the sound of its breathing.
The dark drinks itself up.

Your kiss is salt and wine.
There's a trick to everything, you say,

pulling aside the curtain. The moon
empties its bucket into the room.

You lead me out under the stars
and begin to count.

Woodworker

To see if they measure up, he sets
one plank beside the other, sights
along the edge, and checks
for bowing. Satisfied, he makes
his measurements and markings,
quick flicks with the pencil he tucks
back behind an ear. I love

a man with the smell of fresh-cut
wood on his hands, who can handle
brace and bit, band saw and blade.
He takes his pleasure in birdseye,
tiger, ribbon, and flame, speaks
the language of heartwood,

a man with an instinct for how much
pressure can be brought to bear
on whatever he touches, when
it will stand strong, when
it will naturally give.

Ode to What Settles

What settles is what stays

after the transience of houses
after the horses and the boulders

particles, dust and ash, leaves
and water after the wind's ruffling.

The fog in the valley, mist on the pond.

What's left when the rest has burned
or blown, what drifts toward twilight.

And after the chaos of yellow windows,
evening deep into the hills.

The silence when you open the door
to an empty sky, the sparrow on its branch.

Our rooms late in the day, creaking
and sighing, the rocker coming to rest

sediment in the bottle, the last of the wine
in the glass

our bodies gone quiet beneath the blanket,
lives into a pattern, knowledge into the bone.

Directions

Intimately acquainted with circles now,
I lean into the curves, take my cues

from the slope of a shoulder, from ruts
and rivulets. the hard-nosed hills.

I've come to accept that a road knows
where it's going whether you trust it or not.

I've forgotten the notion of arrival, so long
a vagrant, stunned and delayed by sun,

distracted by water over stone, the hawk's
hover and wheel, any moving beauty.

If someone should ask, I can say this much:
Turn anywhere, and then keep going.

About the Author

Antonia Clark, a medical writer and editor, has also taught poetry and fiction writing and co-administers an online poetry forum, The Waters. She is the author of a poetry chapbook, *Smoke and Mirrors* (Finishing Line Press, 2013). Forthcoming titles from Bellevue Books include *Dance Craze* and *Why My Body*. Toni lives in Vermont, loves French picnics, and plays French café music on a sparkly purple accordion.

If you enjoyed these poems or would like a free poetry sampler, send a note to antoniaclarkpoetry@gmail.com. The poetry sampler, *Territories*, contains 16 poems from forthcoming books and is available in PDF, EPUB, and MOBI (Kindle) formats.

www.ingramcontent.com/pod-product-compliance
Lightning Source LLC
Chambersburg PA
CBHW021212020426
42331CB00003B/324